XMAS

Norman Ferguson & Mary-Claire Kelly

This book belongs to:

....

PORTICO

First published in the United Kingdom in 2008 by
Portico Books
10 Southcombe Street
London
W14 0RA

An imprint of Anova Books Company Ltd

ISBN 9781906032395

A CIP catalogue record for this book is available from the British Library.

10 9 8 7 6 5 4 3 2 1

Printed and bound by CT Printing Ltd, China

This book can be ordered direct from the publisher.
Contact the marketing department, but try your bookshop first.

www.anovabooks.com

INTRODUCTION

Xmas comes but once a year, as the well-worn saying goes. Which is just as well as otherwise liver disease would be rampant, there would be new levels of unsustainable personal debt, and the divorce courts would need an extension. These days the build-up starts earlier and earlier each year, with Xmas puddings appearing in shops in September. You may even receive an email in February from the office social convenor seeking confirmation of your attendance at this year's bash. And a deposit. And would you like the cock-a-leekie soup or smoked salmon to start?

Xmas as you will See makes outwardly normal people behave in unusual ways. It is the ultimate consumer experience: shops open an incredible 24 hours a day in December. So when panic sets in that the amount of cranberry sauce in the cupboard won't feed a mouse never mind a table full of hungry guests, your local hypermarket is open for business.

The long dark nights of Xmas can cause a certain type of madness. In an attempt to stave off seasonal depression and fear of impending global environmental collapse, some house-owners cheer us up by cranking up the tatometer and festooning their homes with coloured bulbs and inflatable Santas of joy. Unless the green protestors get there first, that is.

There is much fun to be had at this time of year. 'Tis the season for guilt-free bingeing. No one will murmur disapproval if you're swigging port before midday and eating Revels for breakfast. It is Xmas after all! You will also be able to give your creativity free rein by decorating your surroundings with all manner of kitsch objects and working out original ways to sport that Santa suit. There will, however, be payback. January is when millions of detox diets start. And when they usually stop.

HOW TO ENJOY YOUR I SEE BOOK

Use this book as your guide as you approach Xmas, as all this and more can be spotted by the eagle-eyed. Don't worry if you miss anything because, as sure as a drunken embarrassing incident at the office party, it'll all be back again next year. As you see them tick the box and answer the questions. (Answers at the back – no peeping!) When you've finished send a crisp £20 note to:
I See, I0 Southcombe Street, London, W14 0RA
and our staff will send you a certificate with a big 'Well Done!' printed on it.

So sharpen your pencils and have a Happy I See Xmas!

XMAS IS COMING

With the summer holidays barely over it's time for Xmas. Love it or hate it there is simply no getting away from it. As the build-up to the main event continues there are some sure-fire signs that the festival to end all festivals is on its way.

Advent Calendars help the countdown with a treat behind each window.
I See 25 days' worth of choccies. All eaten on the first day

A cart appears on the high street selling seasonal fare.
I See chestnuts roasting by a taxi rank

They're here all year round but robins' breasts will now be Seen more than Jordan's.
I See the Xmas icon: Sir Robin of calendars, cards and gift tags

Of course, for some, Xmas never goes away.
I See 365 days of Xmas for this shop's staff who tend to find July somewhat quiet

Before everyone gets carried away it's wise to heed some notes of caution as Xmas can be a time of tragedy. At this time of year you will See many campaigns urging people not to be reckless or have *too* good a time. 'Tis the season to be careful.

Around 10 million turkeys are cooked in the UK each year, most of them at Christmas.
I See a bird in the sink, worth 2 in the factory farm ☐

Advice is everywhere.
I See the juices running clear, hopefully ☐

As with all things moderation is the key. You don't want to end up like the girl in this poster. Look at those split ends!
I See 12 penalty points and some conditioner ☐

Bargain-store fairy lights, adapter plugs, and candles shaped like Santas can all start the fire.
I See 200 degrees of domestic warming ☐

SOMETHING IN THE AIR

Your first awareness that a certain madness is afoot may come in the form of sound waves through the air. You may find yourself unconsciously humming 70's glam rock tunes. Resistance is futile. These songs will be running around in your brain all day, every day. There is absolutely no escape. It's Christmaaaasss!

What is that tinny racket coming from the boom box?
I See simply having a wonderful Xmas time

They pipe it in through the mall's speakers. If you play some Xmas songs backwards you can hear a satanic voice repeating 'spend spend spend' over and over again.
I See last Xmas I gave you my heart

At any time, a strange apparition from Xmas past may appear...
I See Merry Xmas everyone

Where the speakers cannot go there is room for a brass band.
I See parupa pum pum

Into the short dark days of winter come the bright lights of Christmas, a welcome antidote to the grimness of the all-pervading gloom. There can be no mistaking what's about to be upon us when these are Seen.

THIS TREE IS GIVEN BY THE CITY OF OSLO AS A TOKEN OF NORWEGIAN GRATITUDE TO THE PEOPLE OF LONDON FOR THEIR ASSISTANCE DURING THE YEARS 1940-45.

A TREE HAS BEEN GIVEN ANNUALLY SINCE 1947.

You may notice the large city centre tree near you has been donated by those lovely Norwegians.
I See 'tis the Season of Goodwill, for sure

See the lights first as they appear on trees before the big switch-on.
I See no energy saving bulbs in sight

Children and their parents gather for the switching on of the lights by a 'local celebrity'.
I See a £300 appearance fee plus cab home

These lights will not see a local radio DJ turning them on, but rather a council worker flicking a switch.
I See an angel waiting to shine

BRIGHT LIGHTS, BIG CITY

What a difference a sunset makes...

An upmarket city centre pub before and after.
I See £4 a pint ☐

A provincial town puts on the razzmatazz.
I See low-voltage thrills ☐

I See a tasteful city centre Xmas tree before and after ☐

Don't eat a big meal before boarding.
I See a cheap centrifuge ☐

Many towns and cities adorn their high streets with lavish light displays and not too many people complain about the increase in council tax or the implications for global warming and apocalypse. Can you See the following famous Xmas vistas?

I See a festival city.
Can you name it? _____

I See a northern town where every day feels like Sunday, or Xmas.
Can you name it? _____

I See a Capital Xmas.
Can you name it? _____

I See you Jimmy. And reindeers.
Can you name it? _____

If you find the lavish lights a little vulgar you might prefer them in smaller towns where councils spend budget allocations on health and education rather than on Christmas lights.
I See one shining star of wonder

QUIRKY LIGHTS

Each year brings a greater variety of Xmas decorations and lights, each imparting their own Xmas message. Here is a selection of unusual decorations. See if you can spot similar in your own area.

There is an old saying: 'That's as camp as Xmas'. A 20-foot-high feathered reindeer in the style of a Las Vegas showgirl fits the bill.
I See this one outside a local garden centre ☐

A classic combination of the 2 giants of the season:
Santa and God.
I See both for a Ho-Ho-Holy Night ☐

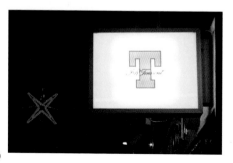

The Three Kings followed their own star to Bethlehem. This star also guides the way... to a different kind of saviour.
I See for 2 pints and a new messiah ☐

Don't get too close! You will often See a valuable street-light adornment guarded by a CCTV camera to protect it from thieves and vandals.
I See Everything ☐

Some locals fed up of parking restrictions convey the spirit of Xmas by transforming traffic cones into a giant star.
I See unrestricted parking on Xmas day ☐

Robins are so Xmassy they poop holly.
I See a sore avian arse ☐

Xmas lights can convey all sorts of meanings.
I See a red ribbon ☐

WINTER WONDERLAND

In the olden days during winter months the rivers and lakes of our towns and cities froze over and people took to them in their skating thousands. Due to our enormous carbon footprints over the past couple of centuries the weather doesn't really get cold enough these days, so instead you may have seen a new phenomenon, the electrically powered city centre ice rink. Don't call yourself a festive city if you haven't got one.

They are all dancing on ice. You can almost hear the strains of 'Bolero'. Roll on the Winter Olympics.
I See for
6.0,
6.0,
6.0,
6.0,
6.0,
6.0. ☐

'Mum, can I go to the ice rink?' Teens love the rink. It's like a roller disco, but with concussion.
I See adolescent boys out to impress ☐

A small ice rink in London is not as spacious as the Thames of old and things can get crowded. Perhaps the council should think about traffic lights.
I See rink rage ☐

Ah, Central Park – the original and the best. As Seen in many a romantic comedy.
I See a New York skate of mind

Where is everyone? On the Ferris Wheel or binge-drinking mulled wine.
I See more space to express yourself on the ice floor

Called 'big wheels' because of their size and shape these Xmas landmarks can be Seen in any town or city claiming the title 'Wonderland'.
I See fear if it starts rolling away down the hill

GERMAN MARKETS

Xmas as we know it was possibly invented by the Germans. Nowadays many towns throughout Britain have their own German Market. They are so similar that we wonder whether a large efficiently run corporation owns them all. Can you See any difference between these towns' markets?

I See Edinburgh ☐

I See Stratford-upon-Avon ☐

I See Bath ☐

I See Birmingham ☐

I See Manchester ☐

It's a Christmas market but not German.
I See Covent Garden ☐

When you See a Xmas Market it will usually be very busy. Once you have elbowed your way through the crowds of other present seekers you might be able to purchase these treats:

Gluhwein.
I See for a £6 a mug. Which may be extortionate but you do get £3 back if you return it. Deal or no deal?

Special Xmassy sausages.
I See things going from brat to wurst

I See creepy wooden soldiers that may come alive at night.

Wooden frogs. Perfect for someone who you've completely run out of ideas for.
I See they make a noise too. Ribbit.

Some more wooden things. Is there a theme here?
I See hand crafted by German elves. In China.

FOREIGN LIGHTS

Xmas is a global event, celebrated all around the world. If you are off on holiday in December perhaps you will see some of these festive lights.

In Italy they keep things stylish at the Coliseum.
I See La Xmas Vita ☐

A huge tree in Brazil.
I See a party hat for King Kong
☐

It's big and brash (not like the people there at all then).
I See a rocking tree at the Rockefeller centre, New York City ☐

In Nagoya, Japan it's cute illuminated teddy bear Santas.
I See Manga Claus ☐

IT'S NOT THE GIVING, IT'S THE SHOPPING

As the nights draw in the enticing glow of the shop window works its magic. Every shop, no matter what it sells, will make an effort to decorate their window display. Can you See any of the following through the hail-splattered glass?

The posher the shop the more elaborate the displays.
I See poor people being moved on ☐

Spot the Santa in this cobbler's window.
I See bottom left for 1, 2, Xmas my shoe ☐

A reindog is the star of this pet shop display.
I See awww ☐

No pressure, with this Barnardo's guilt call
I See for a troubled conscience ☐

Even the local grocers look prettier with some coloured lights.
I See 20 Marlboro lights and some figs please ☐

SPIRIT OF XMAS

The Spirit of Xmas really does pop up in the most unexpected places. A cynic might say that Santa and his helpers can help shift anything. You can make up your own mind with:

The hearth and fireplace expert: Santa. Make sure the fire is out so he doesn't burn his bum.
I See a grate Xmas

The perfect gift: a pair of bifocals from the North Pole.
I See X...M...A...G...no, S

Merry Xmas from your local estate agents. Who said they were modern-day Ebenezers?
I See 2% commission, plus VAT

18

A brave attempt to lift the spirits of those requiring the services of a divorce lawyer?
I See 3 people in this marriage, one of them with a big bushy beard, and it's not Brian Blessed ☐

Even in the midst of grief there's room for fairy lights and some stick-on snowflakes to lift the mood.
I See a ho-ho-hole in the ground six feet deep ☐

It's not their New Year and they probably don't have turkey on the menu but Santa is still there.
I See duck in plum pudding sauce ☐

ULTIMATE CONSUMER EXPERIENCE

Xmas brings the ultimate consumer experience. For some, festive shopping is a pleasure, for the other 99% of us it's like having a grizzly bear in your airing cupboard – you're going to have to deal with it at some point.

It can be hard to find a parking space when the rest of humanity is also looking...
I See just 48 spaces in the entire city

There's always the pavement
I See someone who thinks outside the box

...or impossible at this well-known shopping centre in the North East.
I See someone moving towards their car. Quick!

A kind person has left their parking ticket for the next desperate Xmas parker.
I See the Xmas spirit in controlled parking zone 4

If crowds are your thing head to
the Bullring Shopping Centre in
Birmingham.
I See no one moo-ving too fast   ☐

Retailers feel your pain.
Or at least their staff will.
I See it quieter at 10pm in the
evening. You'd think.   ☐

Avoid inclement weather in a
cosy mall environment.
I See one in a town near you   ☐

When else in the year would you
queue at 9am on a Saturday morning
for a dead bird?
I See no lie-ins in December for the
food cognoscenti   ☐

'I simply must have that
pink feathered napkin ring'.
I See consumers on the edge   ☐

Supermarkets step things up a
gear with a festive display for
every aisle.
I See the colour red everywhere   ☐

With consumer congestion so virulent many use a computer to shop online. This is particularly popular amongst those who live in isolated areas or who dislike human contact.

Looking at dodgy sites can be a distraction from the shopping.
I See Xmas coming early

Even the great man is getting in on the act.
I See redundant elves if this carries on

You can shop online to buy everyone you know a book.
I See 20 copies of I See Xmas

Most importantly, the presents must arrive on time. Post-people carry large bags just like Santa and are the unsung heroes of the online shopper.
I See a Royal Mail Elf in safety footwear with a dodgy back

During the months of November and December many products and services are adapted to include something of the festive feeling. Xmas truly does touch everything.

Even your bum.
I See Xmassy toilet roll

A discarded Xmas-themed coffee cup in a street ashtray.
I See Christmas Blend

'Tis the season to be gambling.
I See all those future debts paid off

Treat yourself or a friend to laser eye surgery this Xmas.
I can See clearly now the pain has gone

BUY NOW, PAY LATER

Xmas can be an expensive time. In days gone by people would save throughout the year to cover the cost. Thankfully in the Modern World it is much easier to obtain credit in various forms. Who can resist the temptation when tomorrow is another year?

A giant TV covered in tinsel on which to watch all those great seasonal specials.
I See nothing to pay for 12 months! ☐

If all else fails there is always cash generator to spread the cost.
I See Xmas cash in hand ☐

Feeling the pinch?
I See money in my account today! ☐

Forget about the kids and their bikes or games consoles. How about something comfortable to sit on?
I See no credit checks ☐

Although shopping is the main focus of most excursions in town, much entertainment can be had from people watching your fellow shoppers. Can you See any of the following?

I See a couple with a present for the little one at home ☐

I See fashionistas on a mission ☐

I See a singleton in the gale ☐

I See a businessman popping out for a bottle of perfume ☐

I See a lady in a red festive fleece ☐

I See a Xmas Big Issue seller closing the deal ☐

I See doing it all at once ☐

I See a romantic moment snatched amidst the throng ☐

I See the burden spread: shop with a loved one ☐

25

DECK THE HALLS

With Xmas fast approaching many households split along the eternal divide: real tree or plastic? The modern Xmas fan may also have to give thought to which is the most environmentally sustainable. The choice is vast but who cares when they look this good?

Conifers come packaged in netting and bright plastic from Northern European countries. It only takes 8 years to grow a 7-foot tree so no worries about burning it in January then.
I See deforestation a go-go

If you can't afford the real thing much fun can be had dressing up.
I See trouble knowing where to place the baubles

If you choose a real tree you might need help to carry it home.
I See a relaxed onlooker having a drink not caring what year it is, never mind what species of tree to get

Much care must be taken in placing a tree in a public place in our health-and-safety obsessed world.
I See a nanny state ☐

Once you've got your tree home, the next decision to make is where to put it...

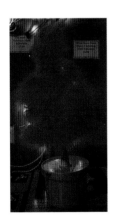

Pink feathered trees may not be available in nature but are becoming increasingly popular amongst radical feminists in the modern world.
I See a girly girl ☐

Is it real or plastic? Can you tell?
I See pine needles in the carpet in June ☐

DECK THE HALLS

Many people have a tree in more than one room in their home.
I See a teenage boy's room smelling of Xmas Spirit

If you live in a cupboard or very small apartment then you might like to convert your light fixing to a tree.
I See how many elves does does it take to change a lightbulb? Ten – one to change it, nine to stand on their shoulders

Keep it modern with a fibre optic model.
I See a low-maintenance Xmas

DECK THE HALLS

Trees can be dangerous for pets and children. And vice versa.
I See a small but determined mutt just waiting for darkness ☐

A small tree still growing in its pot ready to be replanted in the garden come New Year.
I See the way forward ☐

A zany upside-down tree. How does it work?
I See someone who likes to be 'different' ☐

ORNA-MENTAL

Once the tree has been decided upon and installed, decorations have to be added. Some people may have a treasure trove of baubles each with its own sentimental value passed down through the generations. Alternatively you may See some of these, available in all good tat shops.

In case you forget that you're special.
I See a limited production run of only 100,000

Dancing Bear couple with no pants.
I See naked bear in the front with a bear behind

Ouch!
I See cushions on the sleigh

I See bodyless cats looking surprised

Perfect for the mouse in your life.
*I See a tiny woolly jumper decoration
that Stuart Little would like to get on
Xmas Day*

A tree ornament and a chocolate treat
in one!
I See it not lasting till Xmas Day

Still wishing it was Halloween?
I See one for the Goths

Something for the top?
*I See a fairy or is it a chef?
A fairychef*

Or you could keep it simple and
traditional.
*I See 50 red baubles
for 20p*

LIGHTING UP TIME

Once the tree and the decorations are in place, lights can add the final flourish.

Traditionally many hours would be spent untangling the fairy lights which will have been stored in a plastic bag since last year.
I See a frustrating search for the one dodgy bulb ☐

Nowadays many people will choose not to face the hell of disentanglement. Why bother when a fine new set of 100 lights can be purchased from the local bargain store for as little as £1.99?
I See darkness a thing of the past ☐

Some people love fairy lights so much that they keep them up all year round. Or is that just laziness?
I See lights for the design-conscious modern consumer ☐

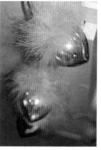

Like most products, fairy lights also come in pink and fluffy.
I See perfect for the girls or fun-loving gentleman ☐

Or there's this tasteful Santa...
I See now that's what you call a headlight ☐

THE HOLLY & THE IVY

In an earlier and simpler time, before electricity and fairy lights, Xmas decorations largely consisted of putting a few local plants about the house. Song lyrics such as 'deck the halls with boughs of holly' and 'the holly and the ivy' helped remind people which plants to put up. Many people still use these plants in the home but have they forgotten the Danger?

Mess with this plant and you might get more than a cold sore. Mistletoe is responsible for fatalities in both children and adults.
I See the kiss of death ☐

What beautiful red berries! 20 are enough to kill a large dog.
I See no safety warning ☐

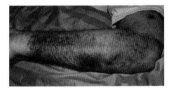

The clue is in the name. This plant comes in poisonous varieties.
I See someone who had an argument with the ivy ☐

The old wives tale says it is deadly to eat this plant but you would have to be very hungry to put a poinsettia in your salad.
I See the Winter Rose ☐

Wreaths are very popular and give the impression someone has died. They might if they eat one.
I See it being OK, it's artificial
☐

PIMP MY HOUSE

Taking their lead from the good ol' USA, the British eccentric has quickly adopted light displays as a form of self-expression, helped out by their local electrical goods warehouse. Around the country many houses are gaily adorned with twinkling lights and figures brightening up the winter night. Unfortunately this phenomenon may not last forever as environmentalists complain about the energy used. Better See them while you still can…

Every town has one, the house where the owner just didn't know when to stop.
I See a surge on the national grid   ☐

An innovative use of those old disco lights from the 80s.
I See boogie nights   ☐

The first sign of what was to come: the ubiquitous icicle light. The real deal is pretty rare these days. Many thought they could stop at this but they were wrong.
I See the full icicle works   ☐

A semi-detached house puts next door in the shade. Literally.
I See an insomniac neighbour ☐

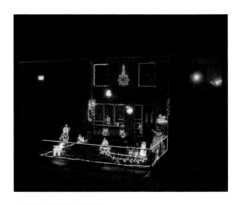

Sometimes the light bug catches on. Here two neighbours have put on a show together.
I'll See your Santa and raise you an inflatable snowman ☐

For some it all seems a bit garish.
I See a tasteful display with no need for the killjoy, busybody council to close this one down ☐

PIMP MY HOUSE

The variety of things which can be illuminated and placed in the garden for public display is endless. Can you See any of them in your area?

Keeping the spirit of Xmas alive in the modern age.
I See a 60-watt baby Jesus ☐

If you are not religious an attractive Santa, sleigh and reindeer combo is a common sight in gardens at this time of year.
I See Donner, but no Blitzen ☐

Just because you live in a council flat doesn't mean you can't participate in the illuminations.
I See Father Simpson. D'oh! ☐

Candle lights give this property a sinister feel.
I See scared children ☐

Locomotives can be Xmassy.
I See lights on the line

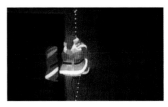

Satellite-dish repairmen can be hard
to find at this time of year.
*Don't worry, I See Santa
to the rescue*

Simple yet effective.
*I See a plastic Santa with
a light bulb inside*

It's your property so make sure it's
protected from thieves and vandals.
*I See smile Santa, you're
on CCTV*

Giant inflatables can be impressive.
I See a fight if it gets windy

Is it Blackpool? Las Vegas? Hull?
*I See a random selection of
Xmassy symbols*

KITSCHMAS

As well as the traditional tree many Xmas fans place ornaments around the house in case they forget for a second that it is Xmas. Many of these items can be purchased for as little as 50p and are a cheap way of giving any room that festive touch. In the past they were known as 'tat' but these days they are called kitsch. Eyes down for a full house of shite.

Hello Boys.
I See camp Santa ☐

His trusty steed.
I See Rudolphina the showgirl reindeer ☐

Let's get physical!
I See a star-jumping snowman ☐

I See Santa's been eschewing the mince pies this year ☐

I See Santa's had a light lunch ☐

I See the closest you'll get to snow this Xmas ☐

'Wot you lookin at?
I See a giant angry Robin ☐

'Please don't burn me'.
I See a Santa tea light with pleading eyes ☐

No chance.
I See torture, Xmas style ☐

The modern office can be a grey and depressing environment. But that doesn't stop determined workers spreading a bit of festive cheer. The approaching holiday and perhaps the prospect of a night out can give an added buzz to those water-cooler chats. If you work in an office at this time of year you may See some of the following…

As decorated by the youth on work placement.
I See a tired tree dragged out from the store cupboard

Impersonal corporate Xmas cards arrive from other organisations.
I See a digitally printed signature, from all at ABC Printers

Work stations may benefit from that personal touch.
I See a Christmas tree wanting to phone a friend

For the Xmas fanatic the fun never stops.
I See an employee who can't be that busy at the moment

THE OFFICE XMAS

If you are out in any town centre you will probably notice lots of incongruous groups of people heading out for their work Xmas party.

I See a gaggle of Xmas partygoers, bonus points if spotted wearing Santa hats ☐

Depending on where you work, you may be invited to a posh extravaganza where the drink is free but you have to sit next to someone from accounts banging on about property prices.
I See another bottle, if I'm going to make it to dessert ☐

Or it may be a more low-key event in the office itself.
I See many refusals to go into the stationery cupboard ☐

A cornerstone of the work night out is the 'Secret Santa'. For some reason the allotted budget has stayed at £5 for the past 18 years despite inflation.
I See someone recycling the same present I sent last year ☐

Shops stock items that are geared specifically for Xmas nights out.
I See a drunken snog with serious repercussions under these babies ☐

Remember not to pass out through over-indulging.
I See a businessman who's forgotten telling his boss where he can stick his KPI's. Until tomorrow morning ☐

If your 'do' is in the office stay clear of the office equipment.
I See somebody getting toner on their arse ☐

Many Xmas parties result in music and dancing.
I See lots of ladies dancing on their own ☐
Bonus for spotting men dancing ☐

For the smokers, facilities are provided for a good moan about colleagues.
I See a drunken diatribe against 'Rudolph' from accounts

If you don't get on with your work colleagues the office party can be a quieter affair.
I See Rudolph from accounts

There will always be one who mixes the champagne, the red wine and the lager with the vodka shots.
I See an unpleasant surprise for the cleaners

As temperatures drop in December the long walk home in uncomfortable sandals can be traumatic and potentially hypothermic. Taxis are scarce as the whole country hits the pub.
I See a speedy escape from Roger from IT's amorous advances

While for many of us the Xmas night out heralds the beginning of a 2-week holiday to recover, spare a thought for those people who have to work over the festive period.

In the battle of the Xmas rota, workers with children have a trump card and most always win. At least for those who do work things are pretty skivey. *I See a young single male office worker with no children, Happy Xmazzzzzzzz*

Those employed to help the sick must also work at this time of year. *I See a medical professional*

It's their busiest time of the year. We'd be lost without them. *I See dedicated bar staff and God bless them all*

Envied for their generous holiday entitlement, teachers do well on the present front too. *I See a teacher's pet*

Merry Christmas
Teacher

43

SEASON'S GREETINGS

Each year millions of Xmas cards are sent. The average person in Britain sends an amazing 50 cards, many to people with whom they have had no contact since last December. It's a bit like Facebook, but with more stamps.

Writing 50 cards can be hard work.
I See a sore arm ☐

I See a home-made card from a creative type ☐

I See charity getting how much? ☐

I See a special giant card for that very special someone ☐

No need to splash out.
I See each costing less than 2p ☐

I See greetings from Tranent.
What county is Tranent in?_____

Short of time? Own a white van?
I See a novel season's greeting ☐

SEASON'S GREETINGS

You will hopefully receive as many cards as you send. It is common to put the cards up for display in the home to show everyone how many friends you have, and there are many ways to display.

For the traditionalist.
I See a mantelpiece ☐

Run out of space in the living room?
I See soggy cards, and a last resort if you've run out of toilet paper ☐

If you are not expecting many this might be ideal.
I See a cylindrical metal thingy ☐

Wherever you are you can show your love for the festive season.
I See Bob Cratchit's badge ☐

DRIVING HOME FOR XMAS

In modern Britain many live some distance from their closest family. Getting home can be the commute of all commutes as the country's transport network is stretched to breaking point. Can you See these on your long journey home?

A friendly motorway sign
I See a subtle message ☐

Long queues at airport check-in.
I See a baggage handlers' strike and a news camera crew soon on hand ☐

A car full of presents.
I See no room for the children ☐

A snowy airport scene. It's not the best time of year to fly.
I See anxiety: have that plane's wings been de-iced? ☐

Travelling by train can be a more leisurely option, particularly if you can afford to go first class.
I See Xmas starting early with a glass of champers at the station ☐

If the budget doesn't stretch to first-class train or even budget airline then slumming it on the coach is an option.
I See 5 hours squashed against a man who forgot his deodorant ☐

If you drive the traffic may be bumper to bumper.
I See Chris Rea on repeat ☐

An inch of snow can cause travel chaos and delays.
I See no room at the travel inn ☐

EFFING OFF ABROAD

There are many reasons why people choose to go abroad for Xmas. In Britain, the weather can be cold and dark leading to seasonal depression. Effing off has the added bonus of keeping you 1000's of miles away from those difficult family members. Assuming you haven't been foolish enough to invite them along.

An enticing Xmas offer.
I See 7 nights self-catering in Lanzarote for under £200!

Unlike most British people, conifers don't like lying out in the sun.
I See the future fate of all Xmas trees

Swap the shopping crowds for the beach crowds. When you're there don't forget to send a picture back to your depressed relatives at home.
I See Bondi Beach on Xmas Day

If it gets too much and homesickness kicks in lie back and think of Britain.
I See a British beach on Xmas Day

IT'S FOR THE KIDS

Xmas is when hard-working parents spend quality time with their children. And once that novelty has worn off, pack them off to the panto or cinema or reindeer-feeding session. The main thing is to keep them well away from toy shops or shops with toys – they might spontaneously combust with excitement.

How about a live Xmas show outdoors?
I See Santa suspended from a crane, in a sleigh made from packing crates ☐

Nearly every town has a panto featuring people who were once famous and those from Equity's panto branch.
I See thingy from Neighbours. *Or is it whatsit from* Home & Away? ☐

Every parent looks forward to the school's nativity play if not to the making of the costume. Just don't take any photographs! A tea towel used to do the trick.
I See a lazy parent's short cut ☐

There's always the latest Xmas blockbuster.
I See them kept quiet for a couple of hours at least ☐

49

IT'S FOR THE KIDS

Children will have lots of ideas about what they would like for Xmas. Usually they will list their demands in a letter to the great man himself. Many children will also get a private audience with Santa, for a small fee of course.

Letters to Santa were traditionally put up the chimney. As the use of fireplaces declines new routes have been found.
I See a magic post box ☐

If a child has been good they might even get a letter back.
I See a very good girl ☐

Dear Nicole,

Oh Nicole you are such a wonderful girl. Every time you smile you break my heart. You are so sweet and kind, I am sure I will be able to bring you all you have wished for, especially your 'Sakura' doll – I hope you have lots of fun with her. You have done brilliantly at your swimming and I am so proud of you. Keep up the good work and I know you are working very hard at those sums – you will get there in the end. Thanks for watching over your two brothers Patrick and Ruairi, they really love you – so do your Mum and Dad. Get to bed nice and early Princess on Christmas Eve – Sweet Dreams Love Santa – You are really special

Santa is kept busy as children up and down the land want to meet with him. Grottos pop up everywhere. Here's one Seen in a garden centre.
I See somebody's dad needing the cash ☐

Now that's a grotto!
I See the corporate child catchers ☐

A quiet morning for Santa at this basic shopping centre grotto. Just a chair in a mall really.
I See the kids just ain't impressed. Waah! ☐

Santas need a break too.
I See him checking the job pages for an 11-month contract position, starting 26th December ☐

Parents and small children will wait for hours to meet him, which can cause tantrums.
I See those little legs getting tired and that dummy being spat out ☐

Santa's little helper looks despondent.
*I See a student wondering if the
festive season will ever end*

The final destination. Having a photo
taken to commemorate the meeting.
*I See no sitting on his knee
these days*

Santa doesn't just live in
shopping centres.
*I See him feeding the
reindeers for free
Go Santa!*

VIRTUAL XMAS

More and more people use computers on an everyday basis. The Spirit of Xmas can be found online too.

Websites allow people to send animated Xmassy messages to cheer up family and friends.
I See Peter the dancing Elf ☐

Email funnies with a Xmas theme give the office worker a laugh.
I See going round the world twice before lunch time until it gets forwarded back to the sender. Eventually ☐

Social networking sites help to spread the cheer, not just by making that party easier to organise.
I See a profile page with a festive tree and jingle ☐

GREEN XMAS

Many well-meaning individuals are trying to get us to enjoy Xmas in a more ethical, sustainable, green, recyclable, environmentally friendly kind of way. They hope that perhaps by buying a charity Xmas card or helping to fund a well in Africa global apocalypse will be avoided.

His sleigh is not powered by fossil fuels.
I See Right-On Green Santa of the future

Cities have set up special markets selling ethical Xmas merchandise.
I See lots of sandals and beards and Santa sacks made of hemp

Young idealists set up a 'free shop' on a busy high street as a counter balance to the retail giants.
I See it not having any Wii's or selection boxes. Pah

Colourful anti-capitalist protestors are an increasingly common sight discouraging rampant consumerism.
I See shop less and live more.
Yeah.

And remember to recycle that 100ft tree, London.
I See 200,000 rolls of next year's Xmas-themed loo roll ☐

You may be responsible for killing a tree but at least you're helping a homeless person.
I See ethical trading ☐

The traditional red Santa hat may be going out of fashion.
I See a green one made from organic free-range nylon ☐

Even some high-street shops are getting in on the act.
I See it's costing something, probably in pounds ☐

In Britain we get through 80,000 tonnes of wrapping paper each year. Some suggest using newspaper instead.
I See the kids' pressies accidentally wrapped in page 3 of the Sun ☐

ETHICAL XMAS

If you really care, give a present that doesn't cost the earth...

Build a bog £50

Forget traditional presents and give a donation to charity instead.
I See disappointed relatives' faces on Xmas day ☐

Condoms
OU2625

Here's a gift with a difference. Male and female condoms with educational materials to make sure that they're used correctly to help stop the spread of HIV. Rubberly jubberly.

£24

"I bought my Gran condoms"

...and she hasn't stopped chuckling since!

It is even becoming common to give prophylactics which will be used in a far-off land.
I See turkey and cranberry flavoured ☐

Shelter

Do your Christmas shopping at a well-known high-street charity shop.
I See money well spent on recycled presents ☐

in Scotla

The postage must be high for these gifts.
I See a pig destined for sunnier climes ☐

When you are done shopping why not get home using a green form of transport?
I See they're not much use since the planet warmed up ☐

I'M DREAMING OF A WHITE XMAS

In days gone by snow was a common occurrence at Xmas. In Hollywood movies it still is. But because the planet is warming up, snow is now a rare sight at modern Xmas. Sorry to shatter those dreams, Bing.

Look how big the icicles were in Bognor Regis in 1974.
I See a woolly mammoth hiding behind these ☐

Much fun can be had fashioning men from snow.
I See what about the women? Sexist. ☐

These days, even a smattering of snow leads to much excitement.
I See what is this strange white powder that falleth from the sky? ☐

Humans are very resourceful. Although the real thing may be hard to come by they have invented a purchasable alternative.
I See use this to create your own winter scene ☐

THE PERFECT PRESENT

Ever since the three kings first turned up with gold, frankincense and myrrh, presents have been an integral part of Xmas. Some say that the act of giving is much more special than receiving. But be careful: testing this theory out by not getting them anything in return can end in tears.

Helpfully, gift shops are now to be found every couple of yards selling pointless items.
I See lavender-scented spoon covers ☐

Xmas presents are commonly wrapped in bright gift paper, sometimes more expensive than the gift inside.
I See where the hell does this sticky tape roll begin? ☐

Traditionally presents are placed under the tree until the big day where speculation as to their contents can run riot.
I See lots of surreptitious shaking ☐

Disappointment can be hard to disguise so practise your 'happy and surprised' face in the run-up.
I See not the desired effect ☐

Many presents for men focus on two key areas: drink and sport.

A practical present for the man who likes a drink or 4.
I See over-packaged, over-priced beer ☐

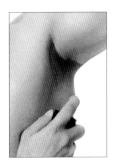

Everyone can smell like a sporting hero with handy deodorant gift sets.
I Smell David Beckham, or is it Wayne Rooney ☐

Combine your man's passions.
I See the 19th hole in your living room at Xmas ☐

How about some bottles to put the drink in when trekking up a mountain?
I See they prevent dehydration ☐

If your man doesn't drink and isn't into sports then he probably has lots of time for DIY.
I See dad being blown away by his present
☐

GADGET MAN

Men like gadgets. If inspiration fails, something with buttons and a 300-page instruction manual to ignore is always a winner.

The bigger the better.
I See an extension needed to fit this inside the house ☐

A device to shout at for giving the wrong directions.
I See at the next junction, turn right. ☐

Wow them with an mp3-playing toilet roll dispenser.
I See a bum note ☐

This gadget is useful for getting your way at team meetings.
I See Xmas-terminate ☐

Possibly the hardest category to buy for is the gentleman of a certain vintage. As a consequence people fall back on various well-worn favourites.

A tactful way of highlighting unsightly nasal hair without actually saying anything.
I See strange trimmings in the sink ☐

If you are a man and you find these in your stocking you are officially past middle age. Sorry.
I See you at least having toasty feet ☐

Remind them of their younger days with a retro aftershave.
I See the scent of Xmas past splashed all over ☐

Like a good malt men may get better with age, although they don't look quite as good if you keep them in a port barrel for 18 years.
I See the water of life brightening up anyone's Xmas day ☐

FOR HIM

If you are still struggling to find that perfect present here is a small selection that might give you some ideas.

Don't just give a thing, give an experience that they will never forget.
I See a flight in a biplane, because the hot air balloons were all sold out

If they don't like flying, or budgets are tight, a model plane will do the job.
I See a jealous Biggles

Cufflinks. Some with naked women on. Why? Who actually wears them?
I See Auntie Mabel isn't very impressed

For the metrosexual in your life.
I See a tres stylish man even in the shower

A traditional gift for women is fragrance in the form of perfume. These days, as well as providing entertainment, many celebrities have 'designed' their own perfume.

Who wouldn't want to smell like Kate Moss? You can with this silver packaged gift item.
I See our lawyer deleting a Kate Moss joke

You should be so lucky lucky lucky to receive this lovely fragrance from the diminutive pop princess herself.
I See this one especially for you

Is she Jordan, Katie Price, or Mrs. Andre? It doesn't matter when she's this 'Stunning'.
I See a whiff of silicone and a hint of airbrush

Everyone knows her for shaving her hair off and getting involved with hopeless men, but while the brand name is tarnished, you can have your own Britney Spears 'Fantasy'.
I See the perfect gift for that rebellious niece

PINK GIFTS FOR HER

In childhood girls are indoctrinated into the way of pink. But not all of them like it. In fact many women hate it so be careful when choosing pink merchandise. Whilst for some pink princesses there is nothing more desirable than pink Xmas presents the modern postfeminist might be very insulted. You have been warned.

I See at a muddy festival ☐

The colour won't soften the blow.
I See a pink punch ☐

For the career woman a USB massager.
I See a USB with a USP ☐

How did she live without it?
I See a foot-shaped flashing mobile phone holder ☐

Perfect for that female boudoir.
I See Ugly Betty ☐

I See digital photos of Jenny's hen night ☐

Handbag as big as Santa's sack? Lost your keys again?
I See them with this girlie handbag light ☐

It's not just men who own tool boxes.
I See does it come with a matching belt? ☐

It's pink, it's plastic. Is it a dry-skin remover or a cheese grater?
I See double points if you can work out what it actually is ☐

Still stuck for ideas?

If your loved one gave you a mistletoe thong then she might appreciate this gift.
I See a saucy Mrs Claus

Can be embarrassing for men.
I See not just priests in trouble in here

A present for a certain time of the month.
I See of course you're not spotty

Hair straighteners are a popular gift.
I See just weave and go with hair extensions

If all else fails.
I See a diamonds are forever, not just Xmas

IT'S THE THOUGHT THAT COUNTS

A teddy-bear sleigh and reindeers for just £700.
I See no playing with it – it's a collector's item, darling

For the fiscally
challenged, a £1 Santa
cork stopper.
*I See a £2.99 bottle of
plonk to stick it in*

A specialised latte
spoon.
*I See life complete by
having one*

How about a one-off
piece of ceramic art?
*I See little change from
£500 but no one will be
able to guess what it is
under the tree*

Many people simply don't get round to planning and buying presents for everyone on their list. In this instance, ingenuity may be called for. The choice will probably be limited to what's on offer in the garage on the way home.

They will know that you got them at the garage but it's better than nothing.
I See fresh(ish) flowers on Xmas day ☐

Highly unoriginal from an uninspired last-minute merchant.
I See someone's face not lighting up that much ☐

ATMs are open on Xmas Day.
I See a £20 note put in an envelope on the way there.
Still, money's money ☐

For the car-obsessed relative?
I See you've got to be kidding ☐

FOR THE PET IN YOUR LIFE

Britain is a nation of pet lovers. People include their pets in the Xmas festivities by dressing them up and buying them special presents. Do you think that the pets know what is going on?

A stocking for pet treats.
I See a top cat ☐

Sweet treats for a dog: canine cigars and truffles.
I See perfect for the mutt who likes the finer things in life ☐

The real deal out on a Xmas shopping trip.
I See a dog for life not just for Xmas ☐

Get your dog to dance along to 'Jingle Bells'.
I See ding dog merrily on high ☐

Is this messing with an animal's dignity?
I See a pitiful plea for help in his eyes ☐

Laced with catnip.
I See it dressed up to the 9 lives! ☐

Selecting the right present can be a daunting task. How do you find that elusive 'gift that keeps on giving'? Even the most well-intentioned present can have a less than ecstatic reception. If that Christmas thank-you note is not to be written in blood, it's best to get the tone of the gift just right.

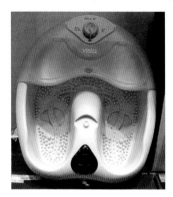

A foot spa can be a useful thing to have around the house, to soak those tired dogs at the end of a working day. *I See a disappointment for someone hoping for a Wii or a new putter on Xmas Day.* ☐

Instead of that romantic surprise trip to Paris or Jo Malone perfume why not express your love for someone with something practical? *I See alarm bells should have been ringing here* ☐

Speaking of dogs, here's a computer accessory that may cause merriment or raised eyebrows on Xmas Morning. *I See it's better than looking at it on YouTube* ☐

If you're past caring what you buy, a plastic reindeer that defecates brown jelly beans could be the very thing. *I See for Number 2 points* ☐

There will be many disappointed children in the world if Santa really does bring plastic storage boxes.
I See I suppose they might come in handy ☐

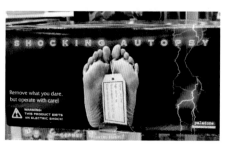

A modern take on that old classic 'Operation' but with a murder victim.
I See for a future forensic pathologist ☐

An interactive game possibly not for all the family.
I See Letch-a-sketch ☐

Each year a new must-have toy emerges and crazed parents give in to pester power and queue up all night in the hope of buying the last one in the country. Toys for children are still largely divided along gender lines despite the best efforts of PC parents. Can you See any of these toys for girls?

Little girls love baby dolls.
I See the caring sex ☐

Cyber girls get hi-tech gadgetry too.
I See the planet being taken over by sinister girl robots in miniskirts ☐

Who doesn't remember when Santa brought their first bike?
I See stabilisers going soon ☐

Computer games and karaoke.
I See fine as long as it comes in pink ☐

If your parents are hippies or anticapitalists you might get a knitted present.
I See everyone else got Bratz! ☐

Get practising for a life of drudgery, girls!
I See Germaine Greer's ire raising ☐

GIVE THEM A GUN

Politically correct parents have given up buying boys non-gender role specific toys.

Boy are made of snakes and snails and puppy-dogs' tails. And a fondness for flatulence.
I See a lifelong obsession

Attention Sci-fi fans.
I See a best-seller never used again when the batteries run out or the plastic bit gets broken

Can we fix it?
I See yes we can

Oh yes, boys will be boys.
I See a toy manufacturer with Deal or no Deal on his mind

Xmas is the one time of year you can eat and drink to excess without guilt. Everyone else is doing the same and anyway there's always the New Year coming when you can clean up your act and start afresh. Given the amount of delights and treats that appear at this time of year you would have to have iron willpower not to indulge yourself completely.

In times gone by the selection box was much anticipated. Nowadays our fat kids see them as a pre-breakfast snack.
I See them but where are the Spangles?

Mmmm, a cream cake shaped like a snowman.
I See 800 calories of pure pleasure

Splash out on something special.
I See a Belgian chocolate Santa with a snow person who looks half-cut

By the end of the holidays huge tins of sweeties will be emptied.
I See even the toffee pennies have gone

XMAS DELICACIES

Mince pies appear in November.
I See them meat-free these days
☐

Yum yum.
I See plum pudding or a 'fly cemetery'. Are there really dead flies in there?
☐

Sandwich shops get in the mood with special festive fillings.
I See a turkey, stuffing, cranberry and bacon feast
☐

You can get Xmas-flavoured soup.
I See it's even got booze in it. Cheers! ☐

Deformed Santa biscuits.
I See in 50 bits by the time you get them home
☐

After all that food you will need to have a good yule log to make you feel better.
I See it's more like a yule cube
☐

Perhaps no other food (apart from Marmite) divides the nation like the Brussel sprout. Love them or hate them you will doubtless smell them over the festive period. Thanks, Belgium!

Inoffensive-looking outside the greengrocers.
I See £1.96 per kilo ☐

Overcooked and tossed in butter.
I See food as punishment ☐

Tossed with some bacon perhaps!
I See anything to make them palatable. Can we beer-batter them? ☐

From our American cousins and sure to catch on soon.
I See Sprout slaw ☐

Did you know they come attached to a branch like this?
I See the axis of evil ☐

CHEWIN' THE GOOSE FAT

It is compulsory for every household to do a very large grocery shop at Xmas. Although the shops only close for a few days many consumers panic-buy staple items such as bread, milk and Stilton just to be on the safe side. Trolleys are piled higher than at any other time of year. At some supermarkets, 'trolley gridlock' may even be observed.

There is much debate about what type of bird to buy. Should it be free range?
I See Xmas turkeys voting with their feet if there's a big enough hole in that fence

Or cheap and cheerful factory-farmed?
I See 2 for £5. That's amazing value and they end up dead either way.

If you really can't be arsed.
I See a festive ready-meal, 8 minutes in the microwave

Dare to be different? Try goose.
*I See as recommended by TV celeb
chefs. Also useful for swimming the
Channel.*

Don't forget the cranberry sauce.
*I See last-minute panic
when stocks are low*

For a starter, try prawns.
I See not life-size

BOOZY BRITAIN

People particularly enjoy a drink at Xmas. It helps to oil the wheels of small talk at the office do, eases the pain of being cooped up with relatives and helps you to sleep through the *Vicar of Dibley* Christmas special.

Some far-sighted people will make a trip to the continent to buy cheaper booze.
I See 9% tasty Belgian Beer and not many sprouts

Bring a festive cranberry note to that vodka.
I See apparently it's very good for the kidneys

Xmas can provide an opportunity to catch up with old friends at the local pub.
I See Rudolph's on the orange juice

For a limited period only: warm, spicy mulled wine.
I See Santa hanging on for dear life

Even garages have special offers on drinks at Xmas.
I See do drink and buy drink ☐

At least this breath tester allows you to drive responsibly.
I See even 1 unit can be risky. Best to live on St Kilda ☐

If driving is not an issue many people will let their hair (and their trousers) down.
I See nice pants
☐

There will always be casualties.
I See the eyesore above ☐

SANTA'S GOT HIS HAT ON

Christmas wouldn't be Christmas without the trademark 'Santa Hat' which is a bright accessory to any festive occasion.

Santa hats are not expensive and can be picked up for hardly any outlay.
I See plenty piled high ☐

Hat technology is always developing and the traditional design has been left behind with this modern Merry Christmas cowboy hat.
I See yee-ho ho ho! ☐

Hats are sometimes given to animals to wear for humorous effect.

I See ... *unamused cats* ☐

I See ... *unamused dogs* ☐

I See ... *unamused rabbits* ☐

It's humans though that hats look best on top of, even if the wearer disagrees.
I See mum and dad not delivering this year's must-have toy ☐

This Santa-hat wearer isn't a human but a mannequin at a saucy high-street sex-toy and impracticable lingerie shop.
I See for 69 points ☐

An unusual twist on the traditional floppy style is this one with the pom-pom supported by a reinforced wire.
I See dare to be different ☐

First name Ebenezer? Not feeling that Xmas vibe?
I See the Santa hat for you ☐

Even Death is in on the act.
I See the ghost of Xmas yet to come
☐

A homeless man selling a magazine.
I See the spirit of Xmas if his stock completely sells out and someone brings him a turkey ☐

Not everyone owns an animal to dress up so you may have to knit your own.
I See Soo the panda at the top of his xmas list ☐

Many people take things a step further and dress from head to toe as Santa. But how can we ever be sure that it is not the real man himself? Could he be Seen in some of these unlikely scenarios?

Not a great example for the kids.
I See a ginger Santa having a fag

The sleigh is broken.
I See Lapland not covered by an all-zones travelcard

Give us the kids!
I See Father Xmases for justice

He's coming to get you if you're not good.
I See a potential source of Claus-trophobia

Fighting a good fight.
I See right-on Santa ☐

After a heavy night out.
I See Santa enjoying some fast food. Hope it's not a 'Donner' kebab ☐

You can See him where you least expect to.
I See Santa at the garage stocking up on Terry's All Gold and anti-freeze ☐

Can you find the real one?
I See an audition for Santa Factor ☐

The King of Xmas can also be Seen in these unusual forms.

Santa in sunglasses on a
Harley-Davidson.
*I See he's 1728 years old and
having a mid-life crisis*

*I See Santa playing air guitar.
We hope.*

Don't do it, Santa!
I See it all getting too much

*I See an inflatable Santa in need of a
second wind*

Hello children.
I See evil chocolate Santa

WORK IT, SANTA!

No mission is too impossible for the big man.

Dear Santa, for Xmas this year I would like a cheeseburger.
I See a side order of fries in your stocking?

I See Ouch! Something's got him from behind!

He abseils down disco lights.
I See the Milk Tray man having nothing on him

No chimney, no problem.
I See this Santa deserving a mince pie

He knows if you've been good or bad…
I See undercover Santa on the job

THE REASON FOR THE SEASON

Many devout people or those just bored to tears by Xmas TV still take time out for a bit of religion on Xmas day and before. The signs are everywhere to See…

A nativity in a garden centre.
I See a cuddly scene. That reminds me, I need a hoe ☐

Remember the reason for the Season.
I See the book of the film, the TV series, the play, the inflatables ☐

It's not just about the shopping.
I See some religious observance with a very berry caramel muffin to go ☐

For churches it's one of the busiest times of the year.
I See a Star is born ☐

THE REASON FOR THE SEASON

A nativity the kids will love.
I See not a bouncy castle so no jumping on this inflatable scene

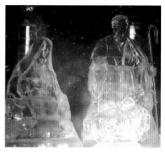

An ice sculpted nativity.
I See it melting into holy water

A beautiful traditional nativity scene in the home.
I See cotton wool instead of straw and gloss varnish to prevent fading

Why not continue the theme with some religious-themed wrapping paper?
I See message received loud and clear

sus Christ Jesus Christ Jesus Christ Jesus Christ Jesus Christ Jesus Christ Jesus C
rist Jesus Christ Jesus Christ Jesus Christ Jesus Christ Jesus Christ Jesus Christ Je
sus Christ Jesus Christ Jesus Christ Jesus Christ Jesus Christ Jesus Christ Jesus C
rist Jesus Christ Jesus Christ Jesus Christ Jesus Christ Jesus Christ Jesus Christ Je
sus Christ Jesus Christ Jesus Christ Jesus Christ Jesus Christ Jesus Christ Jesus C
rist Jesus Christ Jesus Christ Jesus Christ Jesus Christ Jesus Christ Jesus Christ Je
sus Christ Jesus Christ Jesus Christ Jesus Christ Jesus Christ Jesus Christ Jesus C
rist Jesus Christ Jesus Christ Jesus Christ Jesus Christ Jesus Christ Jesus Christ Je
sus Christ Jesus Christ Jesus Christ Jesus Christ Jesus Christ Jesus Christ Jesus C
rist Jesus Christ Jesus Christ Jesus Christ Jesus Christ Jesus Christ Jesus Christ Je
ıus Christ Jesus Christ Jesus Christ Jesus Christ Jesus Christ Jesus Christ Jesus C
rist Jesus Christ Jesus Christ Jesus Christ Jesus Christ Jesus Christ Jesus Christ Je
ıus Christ Jesus Christ Jesus Christ Jesus Christ Jesus Christ Jesus Christ Jesus C
ıist Jesus Christ Jesus Christ Jesus Christ Jesus Christ Jesus Christ Jesus Christ Je
ıus Christ Jesus Christ Jesus Christ Jesus Christ Jesus Christ Jesus Christ Jesus C
ıist Jesus Christ Jesus Christ Jesus Christ Jesus Christ Jesus Christ Jesus Christ Je
ıus Christ Jesus Christ Jesus Christ Jesus Christ Jesus Christ Jesus Christ Jesus C
ıist Jesus Christ Jesus Christ Jesus Christ Jesus Christ Jesus Christ Jesus Christ Je
ıus Christ Jesus Christ Jesus Christ Jesus Christ Jesus Christ Jesus Christ Jesus C
ıist Jesus Christ Jesus Christ Jesus Christ Jesus Christ Jesus Christ Jesus Christ Je

You've had 364 days to prepare and at last the big day has arrived. Unfortunately, unlike France in December 1915, hostilities don't always cease for the day but wherever you are here are some reminders that the main event is upon you.

The cookies and dram (or milk) left for Santa will have disappeared.
I See Santa on a diet tomorrow

If you have kids you will be awoken around about 4am as they ransack the place.
I See those IVF triplets are up early!

An eerie silence envelops the land.
I See empty supermarket car parks but you can still shop online

You may go to church on Xmas morning.
I See a congregation squirming on the evils of gluttony

The newsagents will be shut for the only time this year.
I See Mr Cornershop having a very welcome lie-in

A key focus on the big day is The Dinner. Hopefully you will have remembered to defrost the turkey (if you haven't gone free range, fresh organic of course) or dinner could be supper.

Don't leave Mum to do all the hard work.
I See 2 lbs of parsnips to peel ☐

Give her a hand to set the table.
I See glasses at the ready ☐

You may pull a fair trade cracker.
I See ethically-sourced nail clippers ☐

Then enjoy a slap up meal full of comfort and joy.
I See it taking 5 hours to prepare, 10 minutes to destroy ☐

Or not, if the fights start early.
I See not in front of the turkey, please! ☐

Spare a thought for the veggie, stuck with the nut roast.
I See pass the tofurky

Where there is pleasure, pain will follow.
I See the dishwasher being your best friend

Some disturbed individuals will plunge into icy waters on Xmas Day.
I See death by cardiac arrest or major shrinkage, if you're lucky

For everyone else the sofa does fine.
I See room for just one more sweetie

If you are a teenager you may be bored.
I See I hate you all!

TV HELL

With all that time spent cooped up in the house, too stuffed to move much further than the fridge for another beer, TV takes on another dimension. These days the TV schedules are compared negatively with those Xmas classics of the past and what with thousands of channels to choose from things just aren't what they were.

In ye olden days the Xmas double issue of the *Radio Times* generated almost as much excitement as the latest *Harry Potter* book.
I See your felt tip circling ☐

Some things never change. Gripping stuff. Was it an annus horribilis or an annus mirabilis?
I See switching to Channel 4's alternative Xmas message ☐

Will they ever equal the drama of Den and Angie?
I See the Samaritans' number listed in the TV guide. You may need it after a double dose of EastEnders Xmas tragedy. ☐

As seen on Xmas day, sales adverts litter the schedule.
I See no escape from consumerism. Sales start tomorrow! ☐

IT'LL BE LONELY THIS XMAS

If you are lucky enough to be spending the festive season in the bosom of your family or friends spare a thought for those who have to spend Xmas on their own. For many, it can be a depressing time. At least there are products designed so that those doing Xmas solo don't have to splash out unnecessarily.

I See a frozen roast turkey dinner for one ☐

Don't worry, it's only a toy gun.
I See suicide rates soaring ☐

How about a plum pudding for one?
I See a single tiny mouthful ☐

Celebrate with an individual bottle of cava.
I See not enough to get merry ☐

XMAS ON THE CHEAP

Maybe you're the type of person who doesn't like to spend too much money at Xmas or maybe you just don't have any. Fear not, it is possible to do Xmas on the cheap.

Popular at the house of Scrooge.
I See wow, I could buy half a Santa hat with that ☐

No exchanges as this shop mysteriously vanishes on 26th December.
I See the whole shop worth £1 ☐

Pick up these deely boppers and Santa hat at the charity shop.
I See a second-hand Xmas is a first-class Xmas ☐

One step up from newspaper but not as environmentally sound.
I See it so thin you can see the present inside ☐

Don't splash out on expensive glass-ware.
I See 5 pint glasses doing the job just as well ☐

Or wash that bird down with a can of cider.
I See there's even 13.5%. extra free ☐

THE AFTERMATH: HANGOVER HELL

It's cold, it's dark and Xmas is over. You have the shakes, and shooting chest pains. Are you having a heart attack? No, it's just the Boxing Day Hangover from Hell. Here are some remedies you may See to make you feel almost human again.

Does he look as rough as you feel?
I See succour from the fact that everyone else feels the same and at least you don't have to go to work. Unless you work in retail of course. ☐

Fizzy life saver.
I See hold your nose and get it down you ☐

Bet you wish you had remembered to take your antibloat tablets.
I See nothing a good fart won't cure ☐

A greasy fry-up perhaps.
I See bleucchhhhh! ☐

Hair of the dog?
I See more drink, it is Xmas after all! ☐

BOXING DAY

Once you have sorted your hangover you might wish to join the many millions of people who just can't wait to get back to the shops after the one-day hiatus. Perhaps that washing machine you've had your eye on has a tenner off. Or you need a new dress for the forthcoming New Year's Party. Who could resist?!

The hardcore get there by 10am on Boxing Day.
I See husbands dragged out of bed ☐

It's a perfect time to stock up on cards for next year.
I See it makes financial sense but will you be able to find them in 11 months' time? ☐

This is when it helps to have unusual-sized feet.
I See damn, they never have any 5's in the right style ☐

Half price, even at the fair trade shop.
I See concerned Third World farmers ☐

Previously elegantly displayed sweaters.
I See women with madness in their eyes wreaking havoc in shops ☐

How on earth do they manage to sell clothes this cheap?
At £5 a top, no questions asked ☐

Half-price toys too.
I See a shame for the parents Santa doesn't come on the 27th ☐

A successful trip for these shoppers.
I See cash tills going ker-ching! ☐

CALCULATORS AT THE READY

As the sales progress prices are slashed! They can only be one step away from giving the stuff away for free. There are rumours that much of the sales stock is shipped in from warehouses and was never full price in the first place. We don't know about that, but can you See any of these?

I See Massive Reductions! ☐

I See Absolutely Everything Reduced! ☐

I See up to 50% off! ☐

I See Biggest Sale Ever of woollen goods! ☐

I See no time to waste! ☐

I See 50% off clothes! ☐

I See many items 1/2 price ☐

I See even a sale at the Golf Sale shop! ☐

I See up to 1/2 price on sale! ☐

CALCULATORS AT THE READY

There are many levels of price reduction. Can you See all these on Boxing Day?

I See 15% off ☐

I See 20% off ☐

I See 30% off ☐

I See 40% off ☐

I See 50% off ☐

I See 60% off ☐

I See 70% off ☐

I See 75% off ☐

I See an amazing 90% off!!!!!!!! ☐

A quiet moment amidst the madness.
I See an older gent contemplating that lovely A-line dress he tried on earlier

If you enjoyed the Boxing Day sales why not get up super early on the 27th?
I See forget sleep altogether and pitch a tent outside the shop

Alternatively, why not get out to the beach for a bracing walk?
I See your dog is a-poopin' so time to get scoopin'

Many others have the same idea.
I See building up an appetite for that turkey curry tonight

HAPPEE NOO YEAR!

It is one of the most anticipated party nights of the year. Many organised people will have planned what they are doing months in advance. For the rest of us comes the dilemma of what to do, where to go? Everyone else seems to be having such a good time.

If you fancy ignoring the whole thing and pretending that you are not going to be a year older why not get away from it all?
I See a secluded cottage for rent. Why not hire Straw Dogs on DVD for entertainment?

Lose yourself in a sea of humanity at a city centre party.
I See lots of random snogging at the bells and shaking the hands of New Zealand backpackers

A good solution is to throw your own party.
I See leftover balloons from last year

And don't forget lots of champagne. Or cava.
I See no need to pay stupendous taxi fares, you can just roll off to bed whenever you feel like it

HAPPEE NOO YEAR!

If you have just split up from a relationship or have young children and can't afford a babysitter you might find yourself watching lots of other people have the best time ever on TV.

I See going out might be bad but I'm never doing this again

Wherever you are you will receive a text message from all your friends wishing you a happy new year.

I See I got it at 1.49am cos the netwrk woz crashin, gr8 lol

Whatever you do, make sure you kiss a bald man's head for good luck.

I See some not too pleased with this ritual

NEW YEAR, NEW BEGINNINGS

So that's that. Christmas is over, New Year has passed. After all the preparation and excitement it went by in a flash. Now January, the most depressing month of the year, stretches out before you. Before you go back to work, there are a few things to attend to...

First off you will obviously want to change your life completely.
I See a list of all your faults and ways to change them ☐

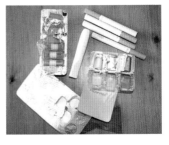

If you smoke you will probably have smoked 1000's of cigarettes in the 12 days of Xmas what with all those parties and stress.
I See you say it every year but this year it's really going to be different ☐

Or place your fate in the hands of the universe.
I See February is especially good for romance but big decisions to be made in the spring ☐

Oh and don't forget to get all those empties down the recycling centre.
I See did we really drink that much? ☐

NEW YEAR, NEW BEGINNINGS

New Year means there's no more putting things off until tomorrow. Tomorrow has arrived. Hopefully the bailiffs haven't just yet.

You will probably have received presents that you don't really want or need.
I See them on an internet auction site. Hope my parents aren't looking for bargains online

Take drastic action.
I See maxed out credit limit

Or if you are still feeling the Xmas vibe do the charitable thing.
I See one persons' unwanted present is another's life saver minus admin overheads

For some people it all gets too much and they feel they can't get through the January Blues.
I See a couple of hours in front of a SAD lamp to cheer yourself up

Just a month ago fragrant pines were welcomed into the home and adorned with bejewelled orbs and fine chocolate treats. Now they have become a source of annoyance, sprinkling their jagged needles into the shag pile and clogging up the vacuum cleaner. With Twelfth Night looming, you know what to do to avoid bad luck.

Stop all the clocks. It bloomed brightly but briefly.
I See someone without green fingers ☐

It might not have been a white Xmas.
I See but it snowed when the trees were put out ☐

Those who are short of time might throw their Xmas tree out of the car on the way back to work.
I See it causing a major traffic diversion ☐

UNDECK THE HALLS

Santa's a bit pooped after all that rushing around.
I See you will know how he feels ☐

Responsible owners are recycling this tree.
I See it trying to escape: 'I want to live!' ☐

This tree has been turned into compost.
I See the circle of life continuing ☐

You may be feeling a bit down in January but you can be sure that by the time December comes around again you will be just as enthusiastic as last time. There is simply something about Xmas that appeals to everyone. Here are some of the more unusual wonders to be found as a taster of what is to come.

For Buck's sake. The singing reindeer. Just £200.
I See in a motorway service station or a hunting lodge

Is it Santa's death mask?
I See double value by using it to scare the kids next Halloween

A soft toy mouse with a hat, jacket and guitar.
I See no trousers though

A Cadillac hearse model.
I See a perfect gift for that death-obsessed goth nephew

All the execs have them.
I See an edible mobile. Also available in Blackberry chocolate flavour

It's hard to tell where the dog stops and the reindeer begins.
I See a real live reindog!

Whatever you do, don't look them in the eyes.
I See a pack herd of reindogs just waiting to pounce

Weird and slightly disturbing.
I See a second head emerging from that Santa hat

Where did I put that wine?
I See it's under this charming Santa wine cosy

A turkey toy with realistic choking sounds.
I See taunting a vegetarian sibling with this

I See a special visitor for a Happy Xmas!..

PHOTO CREDITS

ACKNOWLEDGEMENTS

The production of this I See book would not have been possible without the kind assistance of those who gave up their time, energy, images and ideas. Without them this book would be poorer, although any criticism of its quality and content should not be laid at their door, but at that of the authors.

Special thanks go to: Tom Bromley at Portico who Saw it early and to everyone else at Portico for making it happen; Sandy Buchanan who is generous to a fault; Debbie Strang of Whitenoise Creative Limited who took away a lot of the Quark Fear; RA Ferguson who supplied images we couldn't get; HB Ferguson who had her name in two books and now has it in four; Nicole, Jordan, Peter and Patrick Kelly for being willing models; former Santas PJ and Philomena Kelly; friends and family who when told about it gave great support and encouragement and have entertained us for many Xmases, especially Linda Kelly; Andy Bollen without whom the Give Up option might have been taken a long time ago. Special thanks must also go to the photographers of Flickr and Stock.xchng as well as Wiki Commons, whose willingness to take great photographs of all subjects and release them for creative use has been invaluable.

All efforts have been made to ensure credits are correct at time of printing. Any omissions or errors in accreditation should be notified.

Answers: Bright lights, Big City; Edinburgh, Manchester, London, Glasgow, Seasons Greetings; East Lothian